£ 0.99
14/3

Contents

CW00421140

Introduction and Background

The Norfolk Rising of 1549, which shook the foundations of Norfolk government and society from mid July to late August, caused such alarm to the central government in London, that it was forced to send two military expeditions to suppress it. This remarkable episode in English history is more usually known as Kett's Rebellion, because Robert Kett became its leader, organiser and inspirer.

However, Kett was not a rebel and to describe the events of the summer of 1549 in Norfolk as Kett's Rebellion is equally misleading. Kett and his colleagues sought good government, not the rejection of all government. He led a giant protest against the mismanagement of Norfolk by its ruling class. It was an attempt to achieve a just society not an attack on the State.

The Norfolk Rising was not an isolated event in 1549, though it was unique. The Spring and early Summer of that year was a period of unrest, disorder and riot in many parts of the country. From Cornwall to Kent and from Essex to Yorkshire outbreaks occurred. Yet only one of these disturbances acquired character and cohesion and produced a purposeful programme of reform. This was the Norfolk Rising, and largely it seems, because of the outstanding leadership of Robert Kett.

The causes of the Rising were a complex variety of economic, social, political, legal and religious factors, about which there is continued debate. What is clear, however, is that the town of Wymondham and the personality of Robert Kett, who lived here, provided the place where it all began and the man who became its leader. Wymondham was the stage on which the principal actor would appear and play out the first act of the drama.

Who was Robert Kett?

Robert Kett was born in 1492, the fourth son of Tom and Margery Kett. No contemporary portraits of him exist, although various artists have attempted to portray him. The illustration below is from Ashburton's 'History of England' 1793. It shows Kett at the Mousehold Heath camp under the "Oak of Reformation".

In, his "Life of Edward VI", published in 1610, Sir John Hayward described Kett in the following way:

> *"By bearing a confident countenance in all his actions, the Vulgars (Vassals) took him to be both valiant and wise, and a fit man to be their commander."*

Kett's Ancestors

The Kett family was an ancient one of Danish origin which can be traced back to Godwin Kett in the 12th century. The Ketts had been prominent in the life of Wymondham for several generations before Kett's day. His great-grandfather, Richard Kett had property in Dykebeck and a tenement in Chapelgate. He was also involved in the Guilds, being Alderman of the Guild of the Nativity of the Blessed Virgin. Robert's father, Tom, acquired a property in Middleton in 1492 and he farmed or rented land at Forncett, Tacolneston and Silfield as well as leasing land from the Abbey. He was a butcher by trade and like many of the Ketts, part of the Guild community in the town. There exists a receipted bill by the Brotherhood of our Lady's Light, for the burning of candles at his funeral.

Robert and William Kett

Robert Kett married Alice Appleyard of Braconash, about 1519. They had five sons. Robert was a tanner by trade, but also a substantial landowner in the area. Furthermore he was a leading figure in Wymondham's religious life, being a member of the Guild of St Thomas the Martyr and the Watch and Play Society as well as a server in the Abbey church. His brother, William, one of his chief supporters, was a butcher and grazier – he had land at Forncett. He was also a mercer and had two shops in Chapelgate, near Becket's Chapel and

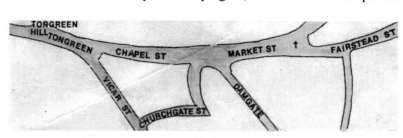

The town centre with the old street names

6

two properties in Damgate. He was an active churchman too, having responsibility for certain ornaments and the candles in the Abbey church. The two brothers therefore, were substantial pillars of the Wymondham community.

Robert Kett's Properties

In many early accounts of the rebellion, there are references to 'Kett the tanner'. Tanning was a vital and profitable business and Kett held the manorial rights for tanning in Wymondham. The tanning process required plenty of water and Cavick, where he had land near the Tiffey had springs, especially in the fields between Lady's Lane and the river.

Property transactions in the 18th century show that there was tanning in Cavick. Lady's Lane, then Wigmore, always figured in the documents. The Tan Vat meadows were almost certainly between this lane and the Tiffey and tan vats are mentioned in these documents. In the 1700s there were three tanners in the area, but we don't know if these tanning businesses were a continuation from Kett's time. One of them had property in Cavick, described in 1752 as including *'two cottages...adjoining in a street called Cakewick Street between the messuage or cottage formerly of Robert Seaman on the east and the messuage late of Robert Kett on the west.'*

Robert was very active in the land and property market where competition was particularly keen at this time. Between 1530 and 1548, when much land changed hands, he was involved in many transactions involving up to 90 acres of land and six properties. At various times in these years, he held land in Browick near Stanfield (40 acres), where he was in competition with John Flowerdew, in Silfield (20 acres), in Suton (16 acres) and six acres in the vicinity of Tyfford Bridge near the Lizard.

He also had 3 acres called Tyffin Meadow. When the Abbey was dissolved in 1539, its lands were sold off and Robert was one of several local men who purchased lands in 1540 and again in 1547.

7

Gunvile Manor

Kett owned various properties in the town, principally on the north side of the Becket Chapel, somewhere in Middleton, in "Ton Green", and at Cavick.

According to the inquest held at the Guildhall, Norwich on January 13th 1550, his property consisted of the Manor of Wymondham, some lands belonging to the Hospital of Burton Lazars in Leicestershire, both, ironically, obtained from the Earl of Warwick, his ultimate destroyer, two tenements at Cakewyk Field near the marlepitts, including some arable and pasture land, and finally Gunvile Manor.

One of the houses he owned in the Cavick area had the interesting name of Wyldehogge. The total amounts to some 50 acres in all.

After his execution, Kett's property was confiscated. Gunvile Manor was granted to Thomas Audley "for his good and faithful service in conflict with the rebels". In 1551 Audley sold the manor to Sir John Clere for £306 13s 4d. The following is an extract from the Conveyance of 20th November 1551:

"All those manors called Meliores Hall and Lethers Hall or Gunvile's Manor and the Manor of Gunviles in the County of Norfolk with the appurtenances late part of the possession of the notorious traitor Robert Kett attainted of high treason and also, all that piece of arable land lying in Wymondham aforesaid in the field called Cakewickfield at Marlespitt containing by estimation one acre. "

Although all of Kett's properties were confiscated at the time of his execution, his eldest son William had a re-grant of some of the lands which had been forfeited in 1551 including Westwode Chapel which had been the property of Robert's brother William.

Why did Kett get Involved?

It is interesting to speculate on Kett's motives. Why did such a wealthy, comfortable, respected and indeed elderly figure become the apparently willing leader of a group of rioters, who in time became members of a great popular movement? Perhaps his involvement in the guilds with their concern for good order, decent conduct and social justice (principles which prevailed for most of the time that Kett's followers were encamped on Mousehold), partially explain his dramatic departure from a life of tanning, farming, enclosing, property investing etc. Perhaps it was his religious convictions and sense of moral outrage at the callous disregard of many of the great landowners of the county for the plight of the `poore commons'. Perhaps it was the provocative action of an old rival, John Flowerdew. Perhaps he believed (wrongly), that the King's Government would support a self-evidently just cause – the

9

reform of a corrupt Norfolk society. Or was it sheer impulse? Did Kett also get caught up in the heady and exciting atmosphere of that summer's day? We will probably never know for certain. However, the personal beliefs and feelings which led him to make his decision were of historic importance. The amalgam of his strong charismatic personality and the discontented peasantry, made all the more determined by the actions of Flowerdew, transformed a disorderly mob into a great demonstration.

How it Started

On 6 July 1549, a large crowd began to gather in Wymondham, to commemorate the occasion on 7 July 1220, when Thomas a Becket's body was placed in a shrine in Canterbury Cathedral. It was also the occasion of an annual fair in the town, two days and nights of festivities, including processions, pageants and plenty to eat and drink. Another event which attracted visitors was the Wymondham Game, a play which was probably performed in the Game Place near the Bridewell.
In addition to merrymaking, there was much talk about grievances. Bitterness and bad feeling came to the surface. In the surrounding countryside there were a number of very unpopular landowners whose enclosure of common land was widely disliked by the many smallholders in the area.

At a time when land was scarce, such men depended on the customary rights of grazing their animals on the common, as they lacked sufficient land of their own for this purpose. It would not take much to stir them into action. Between 7-8th July, some action certainly occurred!
Firstly, groups of the most discontented, went to nearby Morley and pulled down the fences which Master Hobart had put up to enclose part of the common there. Then they set off for Hethersett and began to take similar action against John Flowerdew, "a gentleman of good estate, but never expressing a desire for quiet". Flowerdew was

quick to point out that Robert Kett was also guilty of encroaching on the common land at Wymondham (near the Fairland). He offered 40 pence to the mob (1 penny or less per rioter?) to go and pull down Kett's fences. Then came the great surprise. Rather than resisting the fence breakers, Kett joined in and helped them uproot his own fences, at the same time offering to lead them in their protest. He returned to Hethersett with them where there was a confrontation with his old adversary Flowerdew. Holinshed says that "many sharp words" passed between them. As a result, the remainder of Flowerdew's fences were destroyed.

At some stage during these hectic events, Kett made a speech at his house, indicating his readiness to be the leader of the peasantry. Holinshed says that he "willed them to be of good comfort and to follow him in defence of their common liberty". An unruly mob had found a leader.

Next day, 9th July, a crowd assembled under an old oak on the common outside Wymondham. Here, Kett is reputed to have made another rousing speech in which he said "I refuse not to sacrifice my substance, yea my very life itself, so highly do I esteem the cause in which we are engaged". Then he set off leading his followers to Norwich.

The first stage in the Norfolk Rising had begun.

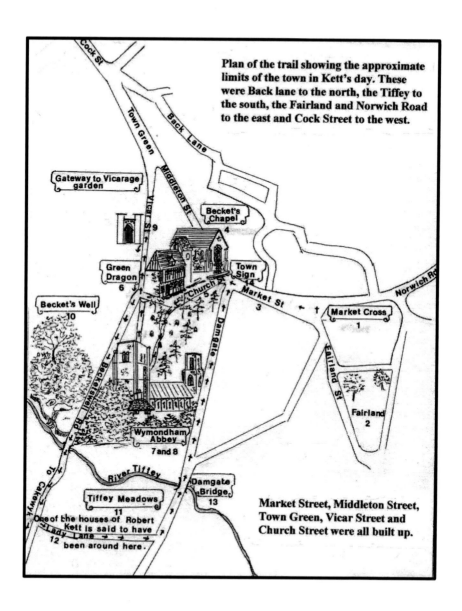

Plan of the trail showing the approximate limits of the town in Kett's day. These were Back lane to the north, the Tiffey to the south, the Fairland and Norwich Road to the east and Cock Street to the west.

Cock St

Back Lane

Town Green

Middleton St

Gateway to Vicarage garden

Becket's Chapel

Vicar St

9

4

Green Dragon

Town Sign

6

14

Church St

Market St

Becket's Well

5

3

10

Market Cross

1

Damgate

Fairland St

Becketswell Rd

Fairland

2

Wymondham Abbey

7 and 8

River Tiffey

Damgate Bridge

Caketwy

13

Tiffey Meadows

11

One of the houses of Robert Kett is said to have been around here.

Lady Lane

12

Norwich Rd

Market Street, Middleton Street, Town Green, Vicar Street and Church Street were all built up.

12

The Trail
(approximately 1¼ miles)

1. The Market Place

This was the heart of the town's commercial and communal life in Kett's day, although the present market cross only dates back to 1618, replacing the earlier one destroyed in the great fire of 1615. The cross in Kett's day was probably more like a small market hall, supporting an upper chamber under which licensed traders set up their stalls. Incidentally, an attempt to continue the practice of building shops under the new market cross in the 17th century was resisted.

The shape and size of the market square is, however, similar to that in Kett's time. Unfortunately, due to the fire many properties were lost and only the timbers of the left-hand side of the Cross Keys are obviously of 16th century origin.

The Cross Keys and Market Square

A view of the "Fairstead" from the Market Square

2. The Fairland

From outside the Cross Keys look down towards the Fairland, part of the extensive common land of the Wymondham of Kett's day. Its name reminds us that Wymondham was allowed to hold three fairs a year, and it was at such an occasion on July 6th 1549, that Kett's story began.

There would have been a lively and exciting atmosphere with pageants, jugglers, tumblers, peddlars, fortune tellers and no doubt plenty of ale! Processions may have passed between the Fairland, the Market Square and the Abbey. Is it too fanciful to imagine that Kett, a member of the Watch and Play Society, was an organiser of some of the plays and festivities at the Fair?

Incidentally, just across the B 1172, Kett had seven acres of land near Tyfford Bridge, land which adjoined or possibly encroached on the Fairland, common to the people of Wymondham. This area formed part of his gradual consolidation of land towards Browick where John Flowerdew of Stanfield also had interests.

Holinshed said that Kett had pasture near the Fairland and Blomefield records that he had enclosed some land near the

14

"Fairstead". Was it here that the fences were pulled down by the mob bribed by Flowerdew?

3. Market Street

Walk down Market Street, most of which was already built up by 1549, but suffered from the ravages of the 1615 fire. Though most of the buildings have been rebuilt since this time later facades may hide older constructions.

In 1549, Wymondham was a real community, a town of some 1500 people. It was largish for the time, twice as populous as Attleborough, Swaffham and Thetford. In Norfolk only King's Lynn, Yarmouth and Norwich were bigger.

4. Becket's Chapel

At the junction of Damgate/Church Street/Middleton Street pause outside this chapel and look at the Kett plaque. Along Middleton Street or Chapel Street as it was called, Kett had a property.

Kett had taken an active part in the campaign to preserve Becket's Chapel, founded in 1174 in honour of the murdered Archbishop of Canterbury, from the depredations of Flowerdew. It had been a shrine

Becket's Chapel from a postcard of 1904

throughout the Middle Ages and was held in genuine affection by the townspeople. Becket was still a popular saint in Wymondham after the Dissolution of the Monasteries and it was in his honour that the great festival of July 1549 was still, illegally, being held. Henry VIII had erased Saint Thomas's name from the Christian Calendar, abolished Guilds dedicated to him and taken away their funds. Often these funds were used to found schools and at a later date a Grammar School was set up in Wymondham, endowed with Becket's Chapel and lands belonging to the Guild of Saint Thomas. The Ketts had been members of this Guild and it has been suggested that on the day of the festivities, the old church mystery plays were performed in this building.

5. Church Street

Formerly known as Churchgate Street, this is one of the oldest streets in the town and led direct to the Abbey. William Kett had two butcher's shops somewhere along here.

6. The Green Dragon

This is one of the few timber-framed buildings to have escaped the fire of 1615. The Green Dragon dates from the 15th century and has a long history as an inn and hostelry for visitors to the Abbey.

Church Street and the Green Dragon

It was doubtless well patronised on the day of the Fair. The shop-style windows suggest it might have been one of the several shops in this little street.

Follow the road round to the entrance of the Abbey opposite the Abbey Hotel. Pause inside the gateway.

7. The Abbey

Kett was prominent in the religious as well as the economic life of the town. He had probably been educated by the monks. He was a friend of the last Abbot and named one of his sons Loy, after him. As well as being a tenant of the Abbot, Kett was a server in the church where he shared responsibility with his brother for certain ornaments and the candles.

After Henry VIII had dissolved the monastery in 1539, Kett had purchased Abbey lands on at least two occasions. Even so, he was a leading figure among a group of townspeople who petitioned the king to let them buy back part of the Abbey church for the town, including the steeple, bells, stone, lead, choir, vestry, Lady Chapel and Becket's Chapel.

Remains of the Priory

The West Tower from Cavick

However this plan had been frustrated by the Crown Agent John Flowerdew, who kept much of the stone, bells and lead for his own use. During the excavations of the Abbey site in 1834-5 a mass of lead (approximately one ton) was found in a cavity below the Chapter House floor. It had Henry VIII's stamp on it and seemed to have been part of that seized by Flowerdew for his own use. Ironically, the king's officers by placing the royal stamp on the lead, prevented Flowerdew from removing his hoard and it was doubtless covered up and forgotten.

The bad feeling that Flowerdew's action generated in 1539, added a new dimension to the existing rivalry between himself and Kett which was to burst dramatically into the limelight again ten years later.

The following popular ballad, reflects contemporary disillusionment with the aftermath of monastic dissolution:

"We have banished superstition
But we still have ambition.
We have shut away all cloisterers,
But we still keep extortioners.
We have taken the lands from the Abbeys
But we have converted them to worse use ".

As you walk towards the church note the remains of the Priory founded in 1107 and the octagonal tower built by the monks.

Before entering the church by the north porch, look up at the great west tower which was built by the townsfolk in the 15th century. William Kett was hung from this tower on 7th December 1549, the same day that Robert was executed at Norwich Castle.

8. The Interior

This can be explored at leisure with the help of the guide books on sale in the Abbey. In the north aisle note the two marble memorial slabs to 18th century members of the Kett family. George Kett, who died in 1722, owned lands in Morley, Deopham, Wramplingham, Hethersett and Diss. In the same aisle, at the foot of the octagonal font, note the Wodehouse arms (wild men of the wood). Sir Roger Wodehouse of Kimberley Hall attempted unsuccessfully to dissuade Kett from his planned march on Norwich. He became the first of the Norfolk gentry to be imprisoned at the Mousehold camp.

9. The Gateway to the Vicarage Garden

On leaving the church, take the footpath running parallel to the churchyard wall and leave by the gate at the junction of Church Street and Vicar Street. Walk along Vicar Street on the right hand side until you come to the gateway to the Vicarage garden. Note the stone arch which is reputed to have come from Robert Kett's house, possibly the one in Cavick. Robert's nephew, Thomas, owned two tenements in this street.

Walk back towards the Abbey down Becketswell Road until you reach the bridge over the River Tiffey. Pause on the right hand side of this bridge.

Gateway to the Vicarage garden

10. Becket's Well

Here the spring known as Becket's Well, rising in private property, enters the river. Before the Reformation, Wymondham was an important religious centre and a place of pilgrimage. The Well was a magnet for medieval pilgrims who believed in its sacred and healing properties.

A view of the source of the spring from the river

Tiffey Meadows

11. Tiffey Meadows

Cross the bridge and the level crossing. In the fields on the left possibly stood the house in which Kett was living in 1549. He had two properties in the Cavick area, one of which was called Wyldehogge. The tan pits (Kett was a tanner) and marl pits mentioned in various documents, could well have been in this area.

The Chronicles refer to a speech, quoted below, which he made on July 8th. One writer has said that the speech was made at his house below the church, situated in a meadow where the tan pits were.

Kett's Speech

"I am ready to do whatever not only to repress, but to subdue the power of great men, and I hope to bring it to pass ere long that as ye repent your painful labour, so shall these the great ones of their pride.

21

Moreover, I promised that the hurts done unto the public weal and the common pasture by the importunate lords thereof shall be righted.

Whatever lands I have enclosed shall again be made common unto ye and all men, and my own hand shall first perform it.

Never shall I be wanting where your good is concerned. You shall have me if you will, not only as a companion, but as a captain, and in the doing of so great a work before us, not only as a fellow, but for a general standard bearer and chief. Not only will I be present at your councils but if you will have it so, henceforth will preside at them. "

12. Lady's Lane

Continue along Becketswell Road until you reach Lady's Lane on the left opposite Cavick House. Turning into Lady's Lane, look at the field on your right which has also been suggested as a possible site for Kett's house.

Walk along Lady's Lane, the approximate boundary of the Abbey lands in Kett's day, with glimpses of the Abbey through the hedgerows. At the end of Lady's Lane cross the railway bridge and walk through the new housing estate to White Horse Street. Turn left into Damgate, the main road from London in Kett's time.

13. Damgate and Damgate Bridge

Walk along Damgate and stop at the bridge over the Tiffey. Near here on the left was the Abbot's mill and in the 1912 floods a millstone was uncovered. A little further along in the Abbey grounds, stood the Prior's house. Continue walking up Damgate. Near the top of the rise there is an attractive view of the Abbey across the meadows by the Old Peoples' Bungalows.

The houses on the left hand side of Damgate were built along the boundary wall of the Abbey. Various members of the Kett family lived in this road at different times, including William Kett. Robert's son and grandson also had properties along here. There are many examples of timber framed houses in this street. At the end of Damgate on the left, the café and Proctor's Shoe Shop were formerly a 16th century inn, the Rose and Crown.

14. Town Sign

At the end of Damgate view the town sign (see back cover) outside Becket's Chapel. It shows the Abbey, so long part of Wymondham's history, with Robert Kett rallying the peasantry under an oak tree.

Damgate Bridge from a drawing by Francis Stone in 1830

Kett's Oak

According to the Chronicles, Kett made a rousing speech under an oak before leading his followers to Norwich on July 9th.

Traditionally, the railed-off tree standing in a lay-by on the left-hand side of the B 1172 to Norwich about two miles out of town is the tree in question. Whether it is of sufficient age is open to doubt.

However in James Grigor's "Eastern Arboretum" a Register of Remarkable Trees published in 1841 there is a description of this oak. According to Grigor, the tree was nine feet in circumference in 1841. He also comments that it was, by that time reduced to a shell of its former glory, but still had a crown of lively green (as it still does today), and should live for many years. Interestingly, Grigor says that the tree was "clasped round with iron" and adds that more stakes were needed to strengthen it against gales. Clearly, therefore, concern to preserve the tree existed long before the 20th century.

Conclusion

The Norfolk Rising began with an illegal celebration in honour of an archbishop who had been murdered for defying his King. It was to finish, with the execution of the manacled body of its leader, who in the end, paid the penalty for defying his King.

Because he was hung as a traitor, Kett has inevitably had, until more recent times, a harsh press. He has been variously described as a "captain of mischief" and of "a cankered mind", as someone who was followed by the "vile rabble", and the "scum and dregs of Norfolk and Suffolk society" and who was "the wicked author of pernicious tumults". To his arch enemy Flowerdew, he was "the bane of his country and the Captain of Fugitives".

However, there are countless testimonies to the strength of his character, both from his critics and his admirers. 'Bold', 'hardy', of 'an unbridled spirit', 'resolute, confident and wise', are qualities which would have obviously appealed to the discontented of his day.

The hostile picture of Kett, which for so long held sway, has been considerably modified with the passage of time and the impact of historical scholarship. In our century, he has been seen as a 'patriot', a 'hero', a 'reformer' even a 'socialist revolutionary' (which he certainly was not). In 1949, the Norwich City Council placed a commemorative plaque at the entrance to the Castle, "in reparation and honour to a noble and courageous leader". This is a fitting tribute to the man who, 400 years before, had thrown in his lot with the less fortunate of his day, and for a few short weeks, had provided a vision of a better and fairer world.

A Drive to Places of Interest Connected with the Norfolk Rising (approximately 30 miles)

Leave Wymondham via Norwich Road and follow the B 1172 in the direction of Norwich. After about two miles, KETT'S OAK can be seen in a lay-by on the left-hand side. Please see the text for details.

About two miles further on the right is the church of Saint Remigius, HETHERSETT. In this parish, Flowerdew's fences were pulled down by anti-enclosure rioters from Wymondham on the day of the Fair. Kett would have passed the church on his way to Norwich. There is a good car park at the church, though the church itself may not be open.

Rejoin the B 1172 and return in the direction of Wymondham. Do not re-enter the town, but continue until you reach the turning to MORLEY on the right. Take this road and drive past the "BUCK", public house and the SCHOOL. Continue until you see MORLEY MANOR on the right. You have driven through what was formerly the Common, part of which Master Hobart fenced off in 1549. He was living at the MANOR and the resentment against his action caused his fences to be the first to be destroyed on July 7th by the men from Wymondham.

Continue along this road, following the signs to ATTLEBOROUGH until you join the B1077 just outside the town. Follow this road, which will take you to NEW BUCKENHAM, round the one-way system noting the interesting church in the town centre. Men from ATTLEBOROUGH had joined in levelling the fences of John Green of Wilby back in June. He had enclosed part of the common land belonging to ATTLEBOROUGH and adjoining HARGHAM.

Continue along the B1077 towards OLD BUCKENHAM and DISS. At the junction just outside NEW BUCKENHAM turn left along the B1113. You will pass a track on the left leading to NEW BUCKENHAM CASTLE. This stronghold with its circular Norman keep, steep ramparts and wide moat was the base of SIR EDMUND KNYVETT who attempted to break up a rebel camp at HINGHAM. New Buckenham is well worth a visit. Return to WYMONDHAM via ATTLEBOROUGH and the A11.

The sketch below is by G. Colman Green in 1909. He also wrote a play entitled "The Squire of Cavick" or "Kett the Tanner".

Curious Norman "keep" in Tilt Yard of Enceinte of Old Buckenham Castle. This charming relic of Baronial Power is one of the few remaining Castles in Norfolk. It has a splendid moat which enabled Sir Ed. Knyvett to keep Kett's men at bay in 1549